Even when a man occupies the most exalted throne,
he still has to sit on his own behind.

— Montaigne

Outhouses

HOLLY L. BOLLINGER

WITH PHOTOGRAPHY BY NICK CEDAR, WILLIAM G. SIMMONDS & JIM UMHOEFER

First published in 2005 by MBI, an imprint of MBI Publishing Company, Galtier Plaza, Suite 200, 380 Jackson Street, St. Paul, MN 55101-3885 USA

MBI titles are also available at discounts in bulk quantity for industrial or sales-promotional use. For details write to Special Sales Manager at MBI Publishing Company, Galtier Plaza, Suite 200, 380 Jackson Street, St. Paul, MN 55101-3885 USA.

ISBN-13: 978-0-7603-2134-8
ISBN-10: 0-7603-2134-5

Editor: Leah Noel
Designer: Sara Grindle

Printed in China

On the cover: Rays of sunlight illuminate this aging outhouse near Porcupine Cabin in Gallatin National Forest in Montana. *Jim Umhoefer*

On the back cover: An Ohio outhouse adorned with parts of a grape vine. *William G. Simmonds*

On the frontispiece: This weathered outhouse in Central New York sports a fishing theme, complete with net. But it also has the most important of outhouse necessities: an old catalog. Its pages could serve as reading material or toilet paper. *William G. Simmonds*

On the title page: When exploring the western wilderness, you shouldn't be too surprised to find an old outhouse. This one, near Austin Ridge firetower in Kamiah, Idaho, still accommodates many a back country explorer. *Jim Umhoefer*

On the table of contents: Once this Montana privy fell into disuse, thriving woodlands quickly erased its path. *Jim Umhoefer*

CONTENTS

DEDICATION

*Dedicated, with
great love and respect, to the life
experiences of Idell C. Tessmer.
I miss you, Nana.*

GARNET MOUNTAIN,
MONTANA
*Outdoor restrooms can have
their rewards, like a view of
the fantastic landscape
surrounding this rugged
outhouse north of Yellowstone.*
Jim Umhoefer

ACKNOWLEDGMENTS

Countless people, throughout many generations, have contributed to this story by actually living the outhouse experience.

My appreciation, in the truest sense of the word, goes to those who have shared their own stories to help complete this book, including Mildred (Heck) Filbrun and the Filbrun family. Thank you, Bill and Andy, for your efforts to keep your family's history alive and your willingness to give new generations of families a look into the journey yours has undergone.

Whole-hearted congratulations to Nick Cedar, Bill Simmonds, and Jim Umhoefer, whose skilled photography and bold creativity captured the images on these pages to show both the intrinsic beauty and disparaging evolution of the vanishing American outhouse.

My immense gratitude also goes to the MBI Publishing Company editors, Leah Cochenet Noel and Lee Klancher, who conceptualized this book and rallied round me in bringing it to fruition. Moreover, Leah, your encouragement, personal support, and professional weigh-in have been invaluable to my efforts.

A final acknowledgment goes to all the landowners, homeowners, and others who have given permission for their photographs, personal accounts, and pictures of their little houses to be published here. Thank you for providing the insider details that many of us modern-day onlookers otherwise only could have imagined from the outside.

*This broken-down outhouse
makes its home in a
small town south of Akron.
Founded in 1817 by German
religious dissenters called the
Society of Separatists of
Zoar, it was organized as
a communal society. Now
an island of Old World
charm, Zoar has many
historic homes that are a
part of the Zoar Village
State Memorial.*
William G. Simmonds

INTRODUCTION

Every great American icon has a lengthy—though not necessarily perfectly maintained—history behind it. From the Statue of Liberty and the American flag to the game of baseball, the hot dog, and even the hot rod. Each reflects certain American ideals, most common among them being the pursuit of freedom and happiness.

The outhouse, though, is a different kind of icon and has a different kind of story—one that represents the harsh realities of survival in the New World and its frontiers. Even in later American history, during the Great Depression in the 1930s, these little houses out back represented hardship. During this era, millions of identical privies were built by the blood, sweat, and tears of those who already had lost everything and then had to swallow their pride and go to work building outhouses. Imagine trying to find morale in slapping together wooden boxes all day, knowing full well that thousands of men, women, and children would literally shit on your handiwork down the road. . . . Although not the career choice for most, at least it was a job.

Nonetheless, our country survived those dark days because we accepted that, as disgusting as human biology may be, we are all people. We are created equal and every one of us needs a private place to pee.

Now, years later, after indoor plumbing has made many of the older generation forget the harsh realities of outhouse life, the outdoor privy has become a way Americans connect to their past, their rural roots, and the time when they felt most connected to the land.

For me, some of my fondest memories come from my family's visits to a small river community close to Pacific, Missouri, named Camp Solidarity, where outhouses reigned. My grandfather, an auto mechanic by trade, was one of the founding fathers of the 50-acre camp—established in 1937 as a "fraternal, beneficial, and educational association."

The land, situated alongside the Meramec River, was planned on paper to be a recreational farm and retirement compound.

But in reality, Camp Solidarity was created to help immigrants of Austrian descent build new lives in America for themselves and their families. During a time when economic uncertainty still loomed, these 50 cottage sites were leased to new camp "members," who had just emigrated from Europe, for lifetime dues of $100 each. In essence, those families who came to settle were able to buy $100 homesteads.

Even as a child, I could sense the esteem people at Camp Solidarity held for my family because of what my grandfather did to help them. So I never minded leaving the comforts of my city home whenever we visited the old country at Camp Solidarity. And even though it always unnerved me a little inside, especially after dark, I didn't bat an eye when I had to face that long concrete sidewalk into the woods to use the facilities.

The camp's primary public restrooms consisted of two rows of outhouses, four on each side. The men's rooms were to the left, the women's were to the right of the forked pathway. The women's row, at least, had one stall with a child-sized seat. That eased my anxiousness a bit because I didn't feel like I was going to fall in every time I opened the lightweight, spring-loaded wooden slat door.

This rustic red privy sits on the property of Pierson's Orchard in Ionia County, Michigan. It has its own white picket fence, which is adorned with colorful corn cobs. William G. Simmonds

The owner of this property
said the main house was
haunted. Dense woods around
the outhouse sustain the spooky
aura. Visitors must decide
which they fear more—the force
of nature or the supernatural.
William G. Simmonds

*Nature is farsighted: she always gives
bigger cushions to people who like to sit.*

A whole community of people used those same outhouses when they gathered for social events and celebrations, and no one seemed to mind much. In fact, I remember always seeing a smile from others I would pass on the path, coming or going, to those necessary shacks out back.

And well into the 1990s, I noticed most visitors still preferred using the old outhouses to waiting in line for the new indoor toilet that the camp eventually installed inside its main building. I guess that's because no one ever really dawdled in those outhouses.

When I think back to 20 years ago, even life at the camp was a simpler time. Today, it isn't as much of a community as a recreational farm and retirement compound. And the outhouses frequented less and less often.

Ahh, the good old days.

Of course, the short stories and tall tales presented in this book are simply pieces of a larger puzzle, one that represents society's perseverance and progress. And while some outhouse experiences shared in this book may not bring about pretty mental images, they're images befitting of what past generations endured.

Yet the lighter side of such necessary resources is pictured in these pages, too. The photographs you'll see here of outhouses from all across the country are visually stunning. They depict untold generations of Americans who, to this day, have experienced and even embraced life without indoor plumbing.

But if you find that you need a reprieve from morose thoughts about what went on inside these little houses, start flipping through the pages a bit. Then you'll be able to better focus on the innate beauty of these scenes we've set from the outside.

In the end, there's no doubt you'll have a better understanding of nature's one true calling—and what to make of your next trip to the outhouse.

DEER CREEK, MONTANA
Years of exposure to the elements have left a black patina on this simple wooden outhouse in the forest that surrounds Yellowstone National Park.
Jim Umhoefer

BODIE STATE PARK,
CALIFORNIA

*Each year this shingled
outhouse moves closer to its
demise. It was abandoned more
than 50 years ago, as was
much of this former gold
mining town.* Nick Cedar

Surrounded by junk, this two-seater also stands in an old mining town. This town, however, hasn't been completely deserted. Randsburg offers visitors a look at the true Old West, with an authentic saloon, post office, and general store. Nick Cedar

GRAVEL SWITCH, KENTUCKY

Penn's Privy looks like it's from days of old, but it was built in 1993. It stands next to Penn's General Store, which has been in operation since 1845 and is still a meeting place for folks from all around central Kentucky.

William G. Simmonds

CHAPTER ONE

Home Away From Home

Each year, the beauty of rural America draws millions of city slickers "back to nature." They come looking for a simpler life, where only the bare necessities seem to matter. Sometimes these urbanites come just for a vacation, a break they savor in the peace and solitude of the countryside. Other sundowners might settle more permanently, buying a second getaway home.

But whether they end up roughing it in a $30 a night campground, exploring the country in their fully-loaded RV, or living in the old farmhouse of their dreams, they look forward to nights filled with fresh air and billions of brilliant stars. Ahh, they take a deep breath and soak it all in . . . until an important question comes to mind: Where's the bathroom?

Many of today's semi-rugged adventurers expect at least a private stall in a well-lit cinderblock-built restroom, complete with mirrors, soap, and even paper towels. Yet often they're lucky if they get four walls and a roll of toilet paper. But that's the beauty in finding life's bare necessities—how much you appreciate toilet paper when you really need it.

When settlers first came to Europe, and then later to the Americas, they handled human waste disposal in a pretty straightforward manner: dig a hole and bury it. Designing buildings to conceal those holes only came about when social order dictated that it was time to cover up the unclean side of human nature. Along with constructing walls and raised seats for comfort came the idea of privacy and etiquette.

Somewhere along their way to exploring and settling the Americas, Europeans lost their sense of smell when it came to tolerating the stench of overfull privies, and they often continued the vile customs of the Old World, such as dumping jugs of jetsam right

RANDSBURG, CALIFORNIA

Decay is working harder on this outhouse than the people who have made a few repairs to it, such as replacing the hinges and doorknob and patching the door.
Nick Cedar

outside their doors and windows. The foul practices of commoners got to be so bad in the more crowded cities, like London, that disease broke out uncontrollably in many places across Europe in 1800s. Even in the modernized Paris, phrases like "Gardez de l'eau" (directly translating to "watch out for the water," but meaning, "watch for the pee pot being emptied out the overhead the window!") became ingrained into the culture's lexicon.

London Calling

Horrific death tolls came as a result of a decade-long cholera epidemic in mid-1800s England, thus creating the need for newly enforceable public sanitation measures, especially in over-crowded London. The problem had become so bad that the thick stench of human waste matted the streets and flooded the waterways. The unsanitary living conditions grew to such an extent that they made everyone in the commonwealth sick (so much so that more than 20,000 Englishmen, women, and children had died from cholera by 1855).

The city had never really worried about public sanitation or adhered to so-called health laws before the disease outbreak. In fact, in those times, it was standard practice to routinely dump chamber pots right outside the windows and doors of every house. People also literally "went" wherever they could do so without public embarrassment, and nobody cleaned up after themselves because there simply was no place to go with the waste. These customs, compounded with the frequency of rainfall in the city that overflowed existing cesspits into homes and businesses, spread excrement and blood-borne diseases like wildfire.

Queen Victoria finally acted on her disgust with the salient sludge that engorged the city's gutters and the Thames River by advocating the construction of a better city sewer system, which helped absorb the muck of more than two million Londoners.

With the establishment of larger underground waterways, including a tunnel that released the flow underneath the river (not on top of it), more sanitary public privies could be built along streets and behind housing complexes. And with citywide drainage available, those who previously threw the household slop out the window could make their daily deposits down the hole instead.

About the same time sewers were being installed in England, America was making strides in plumbing, too. And inventors from both continents soon began devising all sorts of whimsical water closet prototypes and accessories, from toilet paper to bathroom fixtures, to spruce up the new "indoor private place."

Sanitation of the New World

Many of the European settlers who came to the American colonies in the 1700s and 1800s brought their long-held ideas of civilization with them, including behaviors in the area of sanitation. Because many of these newcomers arrived here in part to escape their under-privileged existence in crowded cities, they were unaccustomed to having running water and proper sewer drainage, services usually reserved for the wealthy in their homelands. Yet even though they were so used to throwing the contents of their chamber pots out into

Americans spend the most time on the pot on Sundays and the least amount of time in the one-room sanctuary on Thursday.

The average female spends nearly three years of her entire lifetime in the bathroom.

The majority of people— 64 percent—leave the door open when using the facilities at home.

the streets, they decided sanitary measures were a must in the New World. So as early as 1700, ordinances were passed to prevent people from dumping waste in open townships.

One of the settlers who found out the hard way about the dangers of tainting the local water the supply was, ironically, Dr. Benjamin Rush. According to several plumbing industry sources, the respected physician, professor, and writer had a well in his backyard that many Philadelphians believed had medicinal value, so they flocked to it to drink in hopes of curing all kinds of ailments. Yet when putrid-smelling water from the well finally went dry from over pumping, it became apparent too late that the doctor's privy drained into this basin, contaminating the drink so many believed helped them.

Dr. Rush eventually went on to become a proponent for clean water. He, along with a few of his colleagues, believed that the yellow fever epidemic that struck Philadelphia in the 1790s might have spread due to unsanitary water conditions, not just because residents were living in close quarters.

The good doctor later worked to improve his city's health by pushing for a law to build an arched bridge to reroute a main public roadway over an oft-contaminated creek, where many townspeople gathered water in different sections. When completed, the bridge kept passersby from getting too close to the frequently stagnant pools of the creek that bred mosquitoes and discouraged people from drawing their drinking water there. Thus, a bridge over troubled water improved the health of many Philadelphians.

Prim-and-Proper Privies

Outhouses really gained a dignified existence in the last half of the nineteenth century, the heyday of Victorian architecture. During this era, many high-society outhouses were built to accentuate the political importance or social affluence of the homeowner. Therefore, a typical period outhouse was truly an architectural extension of the main house.

As a result, some of the living quarter's design elements were added to the privy, including shingled rooftops and attractive latticework and trellises. In some cases, the architect created miniature versions of the master residence.

Take for instance Thomas Jefferson's famous Monticello plantation in Charlottesville, Virginia, which the self-taught, innovative architect originally began building in 1769. Built even before the dawn of the Victorian era, the home showcases the elaborate architectural schemes that were making headway into mainstream America. Its design is Jefferson's popular idealist version of neoclassicism, most closely reflected in Roman-style architecture where form followed function. The main house and other buildings have unique floor plans that create intriguing shapes, which also give them extraordinary usability and convenience to one another.

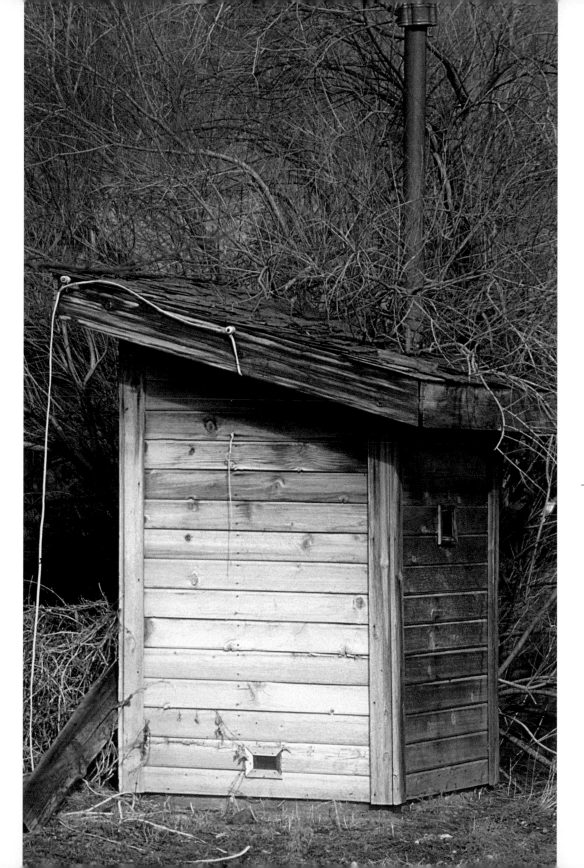

DAYTON, NEVADA
Dayton is an old western mining town and the oldest town in Nevada. The terrain has changed little over the years, including the sagebrush-covered hills that crowd this simple slope-designed WPA outhouse.
Nick Cedar

While scholars continue to study the mysterious indoor privy system in Jefferson's Monticello main house, there is no denying the former president's intentions for his two outdoor privies. Situated at both the north and south ends of Monticello, the two majestic outhouses seem identical. Both are built in a hexagon shape with red brick and conical roofs to match the house. Only insiders knew which one-holer featured a smaller seat for the plantation's younger guests.

George Washington's Mount Vernon is also home to two old-fashioned privies, nearly identical to those found at Jefferson's estate. These two "necessaries," as the groundskeepers still refer to them, have been restored for modern visitors to see but, thankfully, not "visit." They are located on the grounds by the upper and lower gardens.

Government-Sanctioned Sanitation

Most American outhouse designs, however, don't include the fanciful touches of either serious architectural study or a builder's whimsy—at least not according to the U.S. government.

Instead, the top priorities for America's No. 1 government-designed outhouse focused solely on the economical value and sanitary merit of the box above the pit.

Never did those two factors come into play more than during the Great Depression, when, in a matter of just months, millions of hard-working middle-class citizens fell into drastic poverty.

When "The Sanitary Privy" (Supplement No. 108 to the Public Health Reports), was published by the U.S. Treasury Department's Public Health Service in 1933, it highly touted the most practical ways to build, install, and maintain outhouses. The goal of the paper was to urge nationwide construction of new outhouses, following the federally improved privy designs and sanitary measures that represented "the best sanitary privy practices in the various States."

These tips covered the following:

- Use fly-tight receptacles. These kept flies out of the privy, preventing contamination between the privy and home, where flies often roamed, depositing their processed "meals" from the night before.
- Find the best location. This guidance instructed builders so that they could avoid building an outhouse that drained into nearby water supplies.
- Use the best construction methods and materials. Better building practices meant that the outhouse would last longer.
- Learn the principles and means for good ventilation.
- Keep up your outhouse's maintenance. Proper maintenance kept the privy up to parity.

Most of the utilitarian-style outhouses that are still around were born in the Depression era, in part because President Franklin Roosevelt's New Deal–era policies directly funded the mass production of these shacks out back. Through his creation of the Works Progress

Administration (WPA), an entire workforce of "privy specialists" did nothing but build outhouses, constructing more than 2.3 million outdoor privies in just 12 years.

The conceptual design for these mostly single-hole outhouses was the same. A basic frame that formed a 3 1/2 foot by 3 1/2 foot box sat over a pit of the same shape, with a depth of 4 1/2 feet. The outhouse was covered with a slant-back metal roof whereby the front of the privy stood 6 feet, 6 inches tall and the rear only 5 feet, 5 inches tall. The rafters of the roof extended beyond the walls by 5 inches to allow for screened-in ventilation around the top edge and that helped the user to escape rainfall. The doors were standard at 2 feet wide and 6 feet, 6 inches tall. Every outhouse sat on either a concrete or a wooden slab and riser to keep it sturdily elevated above the pit, in case the little house itself shifted.

But the government's design was by no means the only way to build a sound outhouse. Many people took the basic concept of the privy box further, by adding pitched roofs and siding. And the meager frame of standard outhouses didn't provide very much room to move (or breathe for that matter). So a shed-style emerged, with a wider frame that provided room inside for another seat and to store some of the outhouse essentials, such as reading materials and a bucket of powdered lime.

Some outhouses were constructed of material identical to the main house to better blend in, especially those that were in closer proximity to the master dwelling. For instance, brick outhouses are most commonly found not very far from, and sometimes connected, to brick houses.

CENTRAL NEW YORK

Despite their humble purpose, privies accompanying elegant homes often incorporate the same architectural details and craftsmanship used on the main manor. This cross-gabled Victorian loo, painted to match the home, now serves as a garden shed.
William G. Simmonds

CENTRAL NEW YORK
The fine woodwork and gingerbread trim on this Victorian outhouse has a unique style. The owner has moved it from the backyard to near the end of the driveway, where it is used for storage.
William G. Simmonds

George Washington's Mount Vernon estate includes two hexagonal "necessaries," or outdoor privies. Mr. Washington may have considered some of the most important issues of his time in these narrow confines.
Jim Umhoefer

I would rather sit on a pumpkin, and have it all to myself, than to be crowded on a velvet cushion.

— Henry David Thoreau

PHELPS, NEW YORK

Two-story outhouses are rare, and this one is even more unique as it is attached to a well-preserved historic home. Built in 1869, this home is now the property of The Phelps Community Historical Society of Phelps, New York. Its connecting outhouse has entrances on both floors and three-hole toilets on each level—no waiting.
William G. Simmonds

Just because you live in a modern home doesn't mean you can't have an old-fashioned privy out back. The homeowner here made an outhouse the centerpiece of her flower garden.
William G. Simmonds

STOCKERTON,
PENNSYLVANIA

This red outhouse has a unique architectural style with a high wall on the front and a steep roof dropping to a more typical-height wall in back.
William G. Simmonds

26

There is no need to go to India or anywhere else to find peace.
You will find that deep place of silence right in your room,
your garden, or even your bathtub.

— Elisabeth Kubler-Ross

AUSTINBURG, OHIO
This once stately Victorian privy is need of repairs. In its prime, it was a big 12-seater. Now it's being overtaken by the surrounding gardens.
William G. Simmonds

CEDAR LAKE, MICHIGAN
A bridge once connected this rare two-story outhouse to a hotel. The hotel is long gone, but the double-decker privy still stands after more than 100 years.
William G. Simmonds

29

DUBOIS, WYOMING
Timber was the material of choice for early construction in the ranch town of Dubois, Wyoming, founded around 1866. This structure isn't much of a fort, but it does serve a basic necessity. Jim Umhoefer

Do you want an original privy for your backyard? Here's one you can purchase for a mere $2,500. It comes complete with a good window view and lobster trap buoys.
William G. Simmonds

Survival of the Fittest

More than 70 Hours in the Outhouse

An outhouse's design has always been important to its immediate stability and safety. However, after withstanding the test of many years' time, even the most well-built privy can succumb to age and the elements. This happened just a handful of years ago, unfortunately, at the same time a 76-year-old Virginia man sat inside his outhouse.

Coolidge Winesett, a World War II combat veteran and noted mountain fiddler, is now better known in his home state as "the man who fell in" after he broke through the floor of his dilapidated outhouse in Ivanhoe. Clinging to life by only a mud wall and splintered floorboards, Coolidge spent nearly three days suspended above the backyard abyss of his privy pit in August 2000. He was only discovered after a 44-year-old postal worker noticed Coolidge's mail was piling up and went looking around the house for him. A *USA Today* article that reported the incident best describes what happened next—when the heroic mailman "found his favorite fiddler wedged a few perilous feet above a foul smell."

Coolidge's story drew nationwide attention to the plight of America's poor, especially because he was among the eight percent of Ivanhoe's residents that either couldn't afford homes with running water or still had homes with dirt floors. As a result of his harrowing experience, he eventually received a new $68,000 house, complete with indoor facilities. His outhouse-free home was built through the nonprofit Southeast Rural Community Assistance Project and furnished to his liking with the help of donations from people all across the country. Now Coolidge's new single-story home stands right where his turn-of-the-twentieth-century house was falling down.

Since the 1990s, government grants and nonprofit agencies have funded renovation and new construction of houses for more than half of the languishing rural households, like Coolidge's. But the 2000 U.S. Census documented that people in every state continue to live without indoor plumbing.

Many cannot afford the cost of piping water into their homes, running drain lines that can accommodate waste and ventilation, and then connecting to public sewers or constructing septic systems that meet county codes. Then again, a small number of prosperous rural communities choose not to have modern utilities. For richer and poorer, the outhouse is as much a part of these folks' daily routine as the flushbox is to the rest of us.

MICHIGAN

*The dog knows on which side of
this outhouse to stand. Once the
walls start to lean, gravity
exploits the weakness, pulling
old privies down with help
from wind and decay.*
William G. Simmonds

33

SANBORN, MINNESOTA
When Laura Ingalls Wilder's family moved from the Kansas prairie to Minnesota's Walnut Grove, they lived in a home made of sod. This sod outhouse isn't far from the little town made famous by Wilder's books and The Little House on the Prairie *television series.*
Jim Umhoefer

FORT SISSETON,
SOUTH DAKOTA

*This small outhouse on a
historic military outpost was
anything but luxurious. Barely
tall enough to accommodate its
visitors, it probably was not a
favorite among the women who
were supposed to use it.*
Jim Umhoefer

DARWIN, CALIFORNIA
(right) Darwin, California, went from boomtown to ghost town in the late 1800s, when miners rushed in and then rushed out again with word of richer mines in the Bodie Hills. This mining-era outhouse still looks serviceable, but there aren't many people to serve anymore. Nick Cedar

RANDSBURG, CALIFORNIA
(far right) Many a privy has found extended life as a tool shed, but usually with the tools inside. The wares nailed to this outhouse serve as a distraction and a barrier— maybe there's gold in that thar loo! Nick Cedar

36

FORT CHURCHILL
STATE PARK, NEVADA
Long after many of the West's old outhouses have fallen into oblivion, this adobe john will still be standing strong.
Nick Cedar

We ascribe beauty to that which is simple;
which has no superfluous parts; which exactly answers its end. . . .

— Ralph Waldo Emerson

RANDSBURG,
CALIFORNIA

Wood timbers have now become
integral supports for this aging
outhouse in an old California
mining town. Nick Cedar

What's in a Name?

Many words can constitute modern-day potty-talk, but the terms below have been long handed down and passed around when it comes to outhouse life. Some of these have been around for centuries and traveled from continent to continent. To make it known when outdoor relief is in order, people say they are "looking for," "in need of," "going to visit," or "just heading out to" any one of the following synonymous places:

The Ajax (Medieval English)
Aunt Sue (American)
Auntie (Canadian)
The Backhouse (Canadian)
The Biffy (English slang)
The Chapel of Ease (American)
The Chemical Closet (American—coined by the U.S. Public Health Service circa 1917, along with official building plans that incorporated use of chemicals for decomposition and sanitation)
The Chic Sale (American—came into popular use after Charles Sale wrote the bestseller of the 1930s, *The Specialist*, about the humorous adventures Lem Putt, a professional privy builder from Illinois)
The Comfort Station (American)
The Convenience
The Depository
The Donnicker (Australian)
The Dooley (Australian)

The Dunny (Australian—abbreviated form of *donnicker*)
The Earth Closet
The Easer
The Eleanor (American—slang for Eleanor Roosevelt, wife of President Franklin Delano Roosevelt. Used as a derogatory term for the federally built privies, erected in excess by the Works Progress Administration during the Great Depression. Also known as the "Roosevelt Room.")
The Federal Building (American)
The Gardenhouse
The Garderobe (Old English)
The House of Parliament (Canadian)
The House Out Back
The Jake (Old English)
Jericho
The John (Universal)
The Johnnie (American)
The Latrine (Latin—from *latrina*)
The Library
The Little Brown Shack
The Little House (American—the little house usually stood 100-or-so feet behind the main house)
The Loo (English—thought to originally come from a shortened version of the French phrase "Gardez de l'eau," meaning "Look out for the 'water'," which was used when chamber pot

---

WEST VIRGINIA

One reason outhouses earned so many nicknames over the years is that naming them according to their purpose often seemed a little too crude.

William G. Simmonds

waste was being thrown out of windows into streets below)

The Necessary House (English)

The Necessary Vault (Old English)

The Nessy or **Nessie** (English–slang for "necessary house")

The Nettie (English)

One-, Two- or **Three-Holer** (American–used to describe the most common sizes of the outhouse accommodations. The historic Hooper-Bowler Hillstrom House in Belle Plaine, Minnesota (population 3,721), features a two-story outhouse connected to the upper floor by a skyway. After buying the home in 1886, Sam Bowler built the five-holer to support constant traffic from his wife and 12 children.)

The Outhouse (English–originally meant any usable building or structure outside of the primary residence)

Peoria (American–as in Peoria, Illinois, used throughout the Midwest for its phonetic tie to peeing, "I'm heading to Peoria.")

The Pokey (American–slang from the Old West)

The Pool

The Post Office (American)

The Private Place (English)

The Privy (either Latin–from *privus*, meaning "private place," or English–abbreviated version of *private place*)

The Reading Room (American–coincidentally *Reader's Digest* has been the country's reading material of choice in this room since the mid-1930s)

The Rosebush

The Sears Booth (American–for obvious qualities in softness, the Sears

& Roebuck annual catalog provided reading pages that did double duty as the reader's "paper.")

See a Man About a Horse (American colloquialism for a visit to the outhouse, could also be inferred by "buying a horse" or "a dog")

The Shedhouse

The Shithouse (American–slang often tied into the phrase "built like a brick shithouse")

The Throne Room (English–where the King of England would sit upon his regal throne)

Uncle John (American)

The White House (American)

The Willie (English)

The Woodpile or **Woodshed** (American colloquial–as in "taking a trip to the woodpile" or "going to the woodshed")

KENTUCKY

"Restrooms" usually conjures
a more modern image than
the outhouse attached to this
sign in Kentucky. But
"when you gotta go . . . ."
William G. Simmonds

CHAPTER TWO

Run, Run, Run

Even in today's world, filled with modern comforts and conveniences, the word "outhouse" can readily conjure up a distinctive visual and olfactory memory for those who've had first-hand knowledge of a world without indoor plumbing.

Although those backhouse days are long gone for most of the nation, the outhouse experience has not been forgotten. Broaching the subject among a group of twenty-first century American urbanites, even those as "young" as the baby boomers, can elicit an impromptu storytelling session reminiscing on everything outhouse—from the infamous midnight dash to schoolchildren's Halloween pranks.

Many of society's most unpleasant memories and perceptions related to time spent in the little shack out back now revolve around humor, making light of some of life's more unpleasant necessities. And as the time between those who experienced outhouse life and those who pass down their relatives' stories about it grows, new generations begin trivializing the familiar anecdotes of their parents and grandparents. Instead of dwelling on the historical hardships and discomforts previous generations endured and survived, these younger folks share charming "folklore" of days gone by—as if to say, "Those really are just stories that someone made up." Sure, that mentality has a reassuring appeal, especially when the reality behind the stories is more than a little unnerving.

So it has become that many outhouse tales are retold in the genre of "urban legends," even though few functioning outhouses were ever labeled as urban, and even fewer as legendary. And someday soon the first-hand knowledge of privy necessity may die out, but the chaffing outhouse humor buried deep within the annals of human history never will.

NEIHART, MONTANA
*Many visitors might prefer
watching a TV show to
reading the old standby
outhouse catalog—but a
television set won't help you
when you're out of toilet paper.*
Jim Umhoefer

NORTHERN KENTUCKY
A Kentucky two-seater along
the edge of the woods.
William G. Simmonds

WORD PLAY

Many of today's English-language words were born from shortened versions of their truer meanings. Often unrecognized as phonetic cousins to other terms and phrases, these expressions have become so ingrained in our Americanized vocabulary that we rarely stop to contemplate their verbal beginnings.

One such derivative, albeit little-known and hard-pressed by skeptics, is referenced in the 1980 book by Welling Durst, *Privy, Outhouse, Backhouse, John.* In it, the author shares an anecdote about how the small-town criminal element in early America was loosely incarcerated in years past and even given private access to the privy.

As a result, the jailhouses that still made use of outhouses obviously required around-the-clock guards to accompany prisoners from their cells to the shack out back. Of course, the easiest way for the prisoner to announce a much-needed bathroom break was to alert the guard by calling out in an old English brogue, "Take me to de potty!" So eventually, after many a trip to the loo and back, these 24-hour sheriff's assistants earned the nickname of "de potty sheriffs," more commonly known now as deputy sheriffs. If the story is true, it proves that earning your job title can sometimes closely reflect the most unpleasant parts of your work.

NORTHERN KENTUCKY
*Like old schoolhouses, many
old churches still have
primitive privies out back.
This vine-covered men's room
is located behind the Grove
Baptist Church in Kentucky.*
William G. Simmonds

OUTHOUSE HUMOR

*Recently, an experienced carpenter went to work on a job
building outhouses for a large campground in Colorado.*

*The outhouses themselves were built to be sturdy but with a
lot of ornamental touches. Looking at the fine craftsmanship,
it was hard to believe that so much skill and hard work
could be utilized for a mere outhouse. They were truly
architectural wonders, feats of beauty.*

*They had taken shape in the carpenter's home workshop, as it
was well-equipped with every tool needed to make them so
unique. In fact, in order to accommodate the large job,
the carpenter had assembled them on his deck, which
he raised so the "throne rooms" could be easily loaded
onto a truck for final delivery.*

*As the first one was put together, the carpenter's neighbor got
curious and came over to ask what he was doing.*

*"I'm building an outhouse,"
the carpenter replied.*

"An outhouse?" the neighbor scoffed.

"Yep."

"You aren't serious?" the neighbor responded with a jeer.

"I'm perfectly serious, my friend."

*Now the building of an outhouse didn't seem at all strange
to the carpenter. In fact, he was a little annoyed that his
neighbor was being so nosey. He simply couldn't understand
why his neighbor seemed so surprised by the project, until his
neighbor asked,*

"Don't you have indoor plumbing?

Ole and Lena figures on the doors of this double outhouse play on the area's Scandinavian heritage. This couple are the basis for many a corny joke. OLE: "I ran home behind the bus and saved 50 cents." LENA: "You should have run behind a cab and saved three dollars."
Jim Umhoefer

*Bad weather always looks much
worse through a window.*

— John Kieran

49

PARKER'S PRAIRIE, MINNESOTA

In the farming community of Parker's Prairie, winter runs to the privy frequently meant tracking through snow. Subzero temperatures don't make this a fun trip at all. Jim Umhoefer

SAUK CENTRE, MINNESOTA

Sauk Centre, Minnesota, where this snow-blanketed outhouse is located, is the hometown of writer Sinclair Lewis. When his novel, Main Street, *became a bestseller, folks back home didn't find the book's harsh portrayal of small-town life so funny.* Jim Umhoefer

Every mile is two in winter.

— George Herbert

50

COLOR-CODED CORNCOBS

If you've ever heard (or experienced) the prickly yarn of corncob wipes, you probably fully appreciate the softer, even squeezable, side of modern life in which most people flush without giving a second thought.

Now, any backyard gardener can attest that a corncob—freshly shucked and shelled—isn't at all abrasive to the touch. Then, again, it's not exactly quilted for comfort, especially if it's been drying out for a few days. So many early American households initiated the practice of soaking the cobs in water to help maintain the malleable moisture, making them more user friendly.

The cobs then were hung on the backyard privy's walls or piled in baskets on the floor, lending splashes of color based upon the local corn varieties. But these heaping hues were not merely intended to enhance the aesthetic atmosphere. They also served as early toilet paper, where a visitor wiped first and most frequently with the red cobs—followed only by the paler variety to determine if a sufficient amount of the red ones had been used. Now, doesn't that image make you thankful for Charmin?

MICHIGAN

The corncobs adorning the door frame of this outhouse are merely for decoration; but at one time, freshly-shucked cobs served as a very necessary "accessory" to an outdoor biffy. Before the advent of luxuries like quilted Charmin, these corncob shucks were used as toilet paper.
William G. Simmonds

DAYTON, NEVADA

*Time has taken its toll
on this WPA outhouse in
Dayton, the oldest settlement in
Nevada. Fire was a constant
fear in the gold-rush era,
as parched wood like this is
a flame's favorite fuel.*
Nick Cedar

THE PASSING OF THE BACKHOUSE

The classic poem "The Passing of the Backhouse," a heart-felt remembrance and veritable epitaph for children of the outhouse era, is most often erroneously attributed to Indiana writer James Whitcomb Riley.

Shirley Willard, retired president and chief historian of the Fulton County Historical Society in Rochester, Indiana, attests that she personally accepted a reproduction of the 1949 copyright from Charles Rankin's daughter, Kathleen, into the Fulton County museum's collection. Therefore, the county's citizens give Charles Rankin, another Indiana writer, full credit.

Riley himself was known to have denied the work's authorship shortly after it first appeared on a 1910 postcard with his name credited. In fact, he denounced the work as too risqué. Riley even went so far as to document through his attorneys that he did not write the poem. Below are the some of the lines that stirred his ire:

> When memory keeps me company and moves to smile or tears,
> A weather-beaten object looms through the mist of years,
> Behind the house and barn it stood, a half a mile or more,
> And hurrying feet a path had made, straight to its swinging door.
> Its architecture was a type of simple classic art,
> But in the tragedy of life it played a leading part.
> And oft the passing traveler drove slow and heaved a sigh,
> To see the modest hired girl slip out with glances shy. . . .
>
> . . . But when the crust is on the snow and sullen skies were gray,
> Inside the building was no place where one could wish to stay.
> We did our duties promptly, there one purpose swayed the mind;
> We tarried not, nor lingered long, on what we left behind.
> The torture of the icy seat would make a Spartan sob,
> For needs must scrape the flesh with a lacerating cob,
> That from a frost-encrusted nail suspended from a string—
> My father was a frugal man and wasted not a thing.
>
> When Grandpa had to "go out back" and make his morning call,
> We'd bundle up the dear old man with a muffler and a shawl.
> I knew the hole on which he sat—'twas padded all around,
> And once I tried to sit there—'twas all too wide I found,
> My loins were all too little, and I jack-knifed there to stay,
> They had to come and get me out, or I'd have passed away,
> My father said ambition was a thing that boys should shun,
> And I just used the children's hole 'til childhood days were done. . . .

Outhouse Humor

There was once a country boy who hated using the outhouse because it was hot in the summer and freezing in the winter. Plus, it stank all the time!

Because the outhouse sat a ways behind the house on the bank of a nearby creek, the boy dreamt about one day pushing that danged old outhouse into the creek and getting rid of it for good.

Some time later, a hard spring rain swelled the creek to its banks. The little boy decided today was the day to push the outhouse into the creek.

He got a large stick and started pushing it into the outhouse frame. Finally, he felt a slip of the mud underneath. The outhouse slid into the creek and floated away. "Hooray!" he exclaimed.

That evening at the dinner table, the little boy's dad leaned into him and said they were going to the woodshed right after supper. Knowing this meant a spanking, the little boy stammered. "But, why?"

The dad replied, "Someone pushed the outhouse into the creek today. And I know it was you. Wasn't it, Son?"

The boy reluctantly answered, "Yes, Sir." Then he thought a moment and quickly added, "But, Dad, I read in school today that George Washington chopped down a cherry tree and didn't get into trouble because he told the truth."

The dad replied in a deep voice, "Well, Son, George Washington's father wasn't in that cherry tree."

BARABOO, WISCONSIN
Perfect Pete's Portable Party Pottie looks like something out of a children's story, but it's a working poop-house.
Jim Umhoefer

*All hands won't fit on this
poop deck. It's a one-customer
establishment.* Nick Cedar

57

A Work of Fate—The Story of Andreuccio da Perugia

A fourteenth-century literary masterpiece, *The Decameron*, by famed Italian writer Giovanni Boccaccio (1313–1375) tells the story of several young travelers who take turns sharing tales of intrigue during their 10-day journey to Naples in escape of the Black Plague.

One of Boccaccio's fictional characters engages his companions in the story of Andreuccio da Perugia—a young man who travels to Naples to buy horses but instead winds up heading home the next day with a prized jewel.

The most comical of Andreuccio's adventures involves his late-night trip to the outhouse, a second-story privy shared by neighboring households. Apparently, even in the 1300s, bathroom humor got a laugh. The story goes like this:

It was a very hot night, so, no sooner was Andreuccio alone than he stripped himself to his doublet, and drew off his stockings and laid them on the bed's head; and nature demanding a discharge of the surplus weight which he carried within him, he asked the lad where this might be done, and was shown a door in a corner of the room, and told to go in there.

Andreuccio, nothing doubting, did so, but, by ill luck, set his foot on a plank which was detached from the joist at the further end, whereby down it went, and he with it. By God's grace he took no hurt by the fall, though it was from some height, beyond sousing himself from head to foot in the ordure which filled the whole place . . .

After wallowing his way out of the muck, Andreuccio proceeds to confront the neighbors of the woman who owned the faulty privy. Although she had convincingly claimed to be Andreuccio's long-lost illegitimate sister, she turned out to be a clever con artist, who robbed him of all the horse-buying money he had stashed in his clothes for safe keeping.

In a desperate effort to regain his fortune, young Andreuccio inadvertently joins a couple of local thugs in their scheme to rob the fresh grave of the Archbishop of Naples, buried earlier that day wearing an expensive ruby ring.

. . . And so they all three set forth. But as they were on their way to the cathedral, Andreuccio gave out so rank an odor that one said to the other, 'Can we not contrive that he somehow wash himself a little, that he stink not so shrewdly?'

'Why yes,' said the other, 'we are now close to a well, which is never without the pulley and a large bucket; 'tis but a step thither, and we will wash him out of hand.

'Arrived at the well, they found that the rope was still there, but the bucket had been removed; so they determined to attach him to the rope and lower him into the well, there to wash himself, which done, he was to jerk the rope, and they would draw him up. Lowered accordingly he was; but just as, now washed, he jerked the rope, it so happened that a company of patrols, being thirsty because 'twas a hot night and some rogue had led them a pretty dance, came to the well to drink.

The two men fled, unobserved, as soon as they caught sight of the newcomers, who, parched with thirst, laid aside their bucklers, arms, and surcoats, and fell to hauling on the rope that it bore the bucket, full of water. When, therefore, they saw Andreuccio, as he neared the brink of the well, loose the rope and clutch the brink with his hands, they were stricken with a sudden terror, and without uttering a word let go the rope, and took to flight with all the speed they could make.

Whereat Andreuccio marveled mightily, and had he not kept a tight grip on the brink of the well, he would certainly have gone back to the bottom and hardly have escaped grievous hurt, or death.

So it seems that even after being duped—and dipped—by circumstance Andreuccio's fate was changed forever by a surprising trip to the outhouse.

CENTRAL NEW YORK
As far as outdoor plumbing goes, this dunny in central New York has a lot to offer. Seldom does an outhouse incorporate running water, let alone a full sink.
William G. Simmonds

59

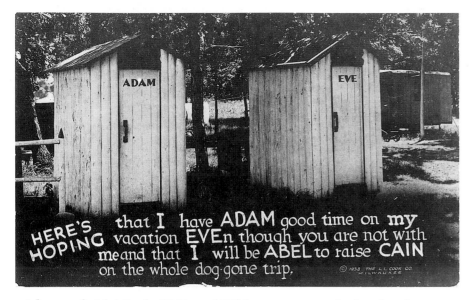

HERE'S HOPING that I have ADAM good time on my vacation EVEn though you are not with me and that I will be ABEL to raise CAIN on the whole dog-gone trip.

© 1938 THE L.L. COOK CO. MILWAUKEE.

(above and right) In the 1940s and 1950s, many postcards played on humorous outhouse themes. This grouping pokes fun at both the Bible's first family and a city girl's case of "mistaken identity." William G. Simmonds collection

COOPER

OH! PARDON ME—
I THOT THIS WAS A PHONE BOOT

No. 21

Here, a postcard with a 1953 postage stamp shows an oddity found only in California—his and hers bathrooms hallowed out of a large sequoia tree stump near the Redwood National Forest.
William G. Simmonds collection

I WENT TO THE GOLF COURSE FOR A FEW HOURS OF FUN BUT I SPOILED MY DAY WITH A **HOLE-IN-ONE**

GC403 ©MWM

There's hardly a subject that golf jokes haven't covered, and as you can see by this vintage postcard, outhouses are no exception. The second card shows that potty humor is older than indoor plumbing—though a skunk seems a better comrade-in-stinkiness than a porcupine.
William G. Simmonds collection

Greetings From THE "WHOLE" FAMILY

DROP-ALL YOUR-CARES HERE

ENTER AT YOUR OWN RISK

-H. DEAN-

RANDSBURG,
CALIFORNIA

Tight quarters for a two-seater.
On the upside, you have an
extra set of arms to hold up the
roof if it starts to collapse.
Nick Cedar

62

Nature gave men two ends—one to sit on and one to think with. Ever since then, man's success or failure has been dependent on the one he used most.

— George R. Kirkpatrick

OUTHOUSE HUMOR

A woman living a rural area wanted to have an outhouse that didn't stink.

After some time, a contractor applied for the job and guaranteed that the outhouse would not have any odor.

He got the job.

Sometime after completing the construction, the man got a frantic call from the woman. "You'd better get here fast!"she exclaimed. "That outhouse has a terrible smell!!"

He rushed over, went to the outhouse, poked his head through the door, and exclaimed, "No wonder it stinks! You pooped in it."

A little more spacious, a little more private, a lot more dilapidated. This one's reached the point where you have to consider taking care of business outside the wall. Nick Cedar

SALINE VALLEY, CALIFORNIA

Saline Valley in Northern California is reachable only by dirt roads. The terrain is largely barren, which comes in handy when you're trying to find an outhouse.
Nick Cedar

EAST ROSEBUD,
MONTANA

*This sturdy brick dunny suits
the ruggedly beautiful terrain
in East Rosebud, Montana.*

Jim Umhoefer

MOUNT BALDY-
BUCKHORN RIDGE
LOOKOUT, MONTANA
*The privy by the Mount
Baldy–Buckhorn Ridge
Lookout is surrounded by the
Kootenai National Forest.
A nearby lookout tower
provides visibility for miles.*
Jim Umhoefer

CHARDON, OHIO
This old leaner in Geauga County is being torn down to make way for a new shopping plaza. But will the mall's toilets be any cleaner?
William G. Simmonds

70

CHAPTER THREE

Midnight Dash

The mere thought of a late-night run to the little house out back sends chills up the spines of those who have had to make it in the pitch-black darkness, sometimes through frigid wind, rain, or even snow.

By the time you got back to the main house, you were awake enough to start the next day. If your internal clock calculated the biology of it just right, you probably could. Otherwise, the insomniac in you might have spent many minutes lying awake, trying to ignore that undeniable urge to go.

In a fondly reminiscent first-person account, Tom Kovach, a baby boomer born in 1945, wrote about this aspect of outhouse life in *Backwoods Home* magazine (Issue 79, January/February 2003) by saying, "In winter or summer, one did not dally long in the outhouse. Growing up in northern Minnesota, the old outhouse wasn't something to look forward to on a night when the temperature outside was sinking to 40 degrees below zero. Even when it is a 'mild' zero degrees, those wooden seats could get mighty frosty."

Born a generation before, in 1915, Mildred (Heck) Filbrun grew up on a farm in eastern Ohio that's long since been absorbed by Huber Heights, a sprawling suburb of Dayton. She vividly remembered her experiences to and from the family outhouse throughout her life. Living with the outhouse etched enough of an impression on Mildred that, at the age of 81, she shared the particulars in great detail for a Filbrun family history book, noting the following:

> Our outhouse, like most, had a half-moon opening cut in the door. Additional small ventilation openings were cut on both side walls. However, these were totally useless, for those little privies were airless and hot as hell all summer and freezing cold all winter. In summer we fought the flies, wasps, and hornets. In winter we often surprised a mouse or an occasional raccoon when we opened the door.

Inside our outhouse were two large open seats for adult use, and a smaller child's seat about a foot off the floor. An old Sears catalog was the only toilet paper ever used in our privy. For many years I believed that toilet paper everywhere was last year's Sears catalog. Our dad told us it had to last until the new catalog arrived.

During the winter months, we kids raced to the privy first thing each morning in our bare feet and nightclothes. Those cold early morning trips in rain or snow were made in record time. Dad told us the snow was good for our feet. To this day I go outside to pick up the morning paper in bare feet no matter how deep the snow. Believe me, that helps you not take for granted your fully carpeted, centrally-heated home!

Tom's and Mildred's experiences were like those of millions of Americans well into the twentieth century. For the vast majority of America's history, living with an outhouse was simply that: a way of life. Indoor plumbing wasn't considered an ordinary feature in the majority of American households, even those near big cities, until the mid-1930s.

The real push to plumb the nation first came to rural America on the heels of World War I during the Roaring Twenties. U.S. Department of Agriculture initiatives, along with those of newly formed trade associations (such as the National Association of Master Plumbers and the Heating & Piping Contractors National Association) developed the first true co-op advertising programs to convince many rural homeowners that professionally-installed heating and plumbing were both affordable and crucial to the nation's progress.

Those organizations were formed in 1918 out of a national committee, later named the Trade Extension Bureau (TEB). The TEB was made up of industry leaders, and its sole purpose was to further the work of plumbers and heating contractors. During the war, the TEB targeted the renovation of factories and city works facilities with advertising campaigns that had just enough of a wartime manufacturing focus that they could pass the federal War Priorities Board's scrutiny.

One of the trade ads depicted Uncle Sam directing a plumber to an industrial complex of towering smokestacks. "Make NEW Business from OLD Factories," it proclaimed. "The Needs of the Nation Include Factory Efficiency . . . Sanitation and Bodily Comfort Is More than Ever a National Necessity."

The series of similar print ads ran not long before Armistice Day and the end of the Great War. Then the TEB turned its attention toward generating demand for new facilities built, of course, with hot running water. It also formulated a mission statement in which it promised to be ". . . devoted to educational advancement so that when peace prevails, America will be the most sanitary nation in the world."

The aim wasn't destined for overnight achievement, though. Despite public interest and engineering innovation, indoor plumbing didn't become a conventional means of sanitation nationwide until nearly a generation later.

In fact, as recently as the 1940s, the U.S. government considered building outhouses a task of national importance. Starting with the Great Depression and throughout President Roosevelt's New Deal era, the federally contrived Works Progress Administration (WPA) trained an entire workforce of "specialists" to build nothing but outhouses. As a result, millions of outhouses sprouted up from coast to coast.

When possible, WPA workers repaired old outhouses, updating them to meet the government's new sanitation standards. These improvements included installing concrete foundations, air-tight seat lids, and screened-in ventilation systems.

If the existing outhouse couldn't be saved, residents paid five dollars for a contemporary wooden one-holer, many of which were supplied through mass-produced potty producers in the South.

Early on in the Depression, the southern economy quickly became America's poorest, but the region maintained its wealth of natural resources, including white pine. Erected with the region's abundant lumber and ample manpower, these New Deal outhouses were pre-built in record numbers by Roosevelt's Civil Works Administration and then shipped by government-funded railways to wherever a potty was needed. By the time World War II had re-energized the U.S. economy, the overdrive production scheme left a large surplus of new outhouses, which had to be deconstructed or destroyed by the thousands.

By the Light of the Silvery Moon

Idell at far left with her stepchildren.

In the early 1900s, in the small German river community of Hermann, Missouri, the "moondivers" earned everyone's respect. But rarely did any of the townspeople want to share a handshake with these professionals. If their social standing wasn't up to snuff, blame it on the moondivers' chosen career path, which didn't make them the best smelling people in town. As a little girl, Idell (Bottermann) Tessmer (1909–1998) was raised in town well aware of the Hermann moondivers' schedule. The town's sanitation and the townspeople's sanity depended on these men to "clean" the outhouse pits on a regular basis.

According to Idell, late at night, usually once a month when the full moon shone its brightest, these illustrious men-for-hire crept in and out of backyards throughout every neighborhood. Armed with buckets, shovels, and strong stomachs, they dug up the worst societal waste from even the best parts of town, proving that at the end of the day all men were created equal.

Idell explained that they always worked by moonlight because no one in town really wanted to watch them work. And in those days before electricity, the lunar glow cast the best light on the subject at hand.

Such an unpleasant job required temperate working conditions, as well. Summer nights were free from the soaring heat and humidity that often stifled daytime air and the swarms of stinging insects usually buzzing around. Similarly, the cold winter winds off of the Missouri River bottomlands tended to die down just in time for the necessary night raid. But the truly icy months usually meant vacation from the profession, that is, unless a particularly talented and determined moondiver chose to don and dirty a very heavy overcoat—and bring a pick ax.

CARSON CITY, MICHIGAN
The farm once served by this
potty parlor on Route 57
is abandoned. Though the
path has overgrown, this
little rest stop appears to
be in solid condition.
William G. Simmonds

*A great, restored outhouse is
on the grounds of the Robert
Harper home, known locally
as Shandy Hall. The Harpers
were the first family to settle
in what is now Ashtabula
County, Ohio.*
Western Reserve
Historical Society/
William G. Simmonds

PARKER'S PRAIRIE, MINNESOTA

This outhouse by Folden Town Hall near Parker's Prairie, Minnesota, is starting to lean. Fending off a century's worth of snow has taken a toll.

Jim Umhoefer

BRIDGER CREEK ROAD, MONTANA

In addition to identifying the small structure at first as a ladies' room, but then later as a unisex bathroom, the crescent moon shape had a couple functions when cut into an outhouse. It allowed light in, provided for air movement, and limited an onlooker's view inside the outhouse much more than a round or square hole would.

Jim Umhoefer

Under the Moon and Stars

There are many theories on the origins of the most popular surviving outhouse icon, the crescent moon. A widely held historical view is that up until modern times, literacy was neither expected nor achieved by many people, so universally recognizable symbols served as the surest form of mass communication.

With the crescent moon signifying Luna or goddess Diana, it became the known as a feminine symbol, therefore welcoming womenfolk. A star, full circle, or starburst subsequently stood for Sol, the sun sign for male.

In service industries where the loo was frequented more frequently, namely taverns and inns, business owners found it increasingly cost-effective to maintain only one restroom. Gentlemen patrons just as often found the places of their calling out back behind a tree. With time, dilapidated "Men Only" outhouses fell away to disrepair, and the ladies' room became the unisex retreat in times of dire need.

Although the original meaning behind the open moon sliver was lost during the Industrial Age in the late 1800s, outhouses across the United States continued to make use of the popular symbol. But these wooden door cutouts, purported to once carry such societal significance, now were used more as a primary source for light and, most importantly, as a vent for fresh air.

CAESAR CREEK, OHIO
One privy here at Pioneer Village has a traditional crescent marking, the other a sun symbol, showing that it's a men's room. Both are surrounded by privacy fencing and are still being used on the property.
William G. Simmonds

OUTHOUSE SONGS

*There was a young man named Hyde,
Who fell into an outhouse and died.
He had a brother,
Who fell into another,
And now they're interred side by side.*

—"Backyard Classic: An Adventure in Nostalgia," by Lambert Florin

WADENA, MINNESOTA

This log cabin and log privy are appropriate for a town settled in 1871. A roaring fire in the cabin would make the bathroom trip more bearable.
Jim Umhoefer

Merry Christmas
and a
Happy New Year

As essential as the outhouse was in the early days, this couple had no qualms about including one on their Christmas card.
William G. Simmonds
collection

Sometimes making that step back out into the snow drift could really give you a wake-up call.
William G. Simmonds
collection

I lived in solitude in the country and noticed how the monotony of a quiet life stimulates the creative mind.

— Albert Einstein

SOUTHEASTERN MAINE

Dimensions of the basic outhouse didn't change much as it moved from the East Coast westward. This narrow-plank john in southeastern Maine is just down the road from the ocean.
William G. Simmonds

*There is something always melancholy
in the idea of leaving a place for the last time.
It is like burying a friend.*

— Abigail Adams

Some old churches still have old-fashioned outhouses out back; others have aging cemeteries. This one in northern Michigan hosts both, as well as a field of beautiful wild flowers. All make the site a peaceful place to visit.
William G. Simmonds

Unprotected by paint or shingles, this weather-beaten privy in upstate New York is slowly disintegrating.
William G. Simmonds

86

Montana is full of rolling, forested foothills for hiking and four-wheeling. This outhouse offers outdoor recreationalists a much needed rest stop in the Gallatin National Forest.

Jim Umhoefer

These outhouses are all on the Eckley Miners' Village property in central Pennsylvania. Because the houses in the village were owned by coal companies for decades, they often didn't see a lot of renovation over the years. That's why visitors can see so many old biffys here. Now this abandoned mining town is kept up by the Pennslyvania Historical Commission.
Eckley Miners'Village/
William G. Simmonds

St. Louis, Missouri

An abandoned building in the Lafayette neighborhood became an outhouse of sorts during the late 1990s for street dwellers needing a place to sit and think.
William Stage

Northern Kentucky

Lush woods await their chance to overrun this collapsing dunny in northern Kentucky.
William G. Simmonds

SOUTHERN MAINE

A couch close by for those who wish to wait their turn. The window height allows visitors to peer out while taking care of business.
William G. Simmonds

RANDSBURG, CALIFORNIA

This dunny sports a wooden seat. It does have a roll of toilet paper nearby, but it looks to be rain-soaked. Where's that old catalog when you need it?
Nick Cedar

RANDSBURG, CALIFORNIA
*Corrugated repair panels make
this loo dark inside, yet they
provide more shelter against
wind and rain than
sparse planks.*
Nick Cedar

RANDSBURG, CALIFORNIA
*This double-ended shack
out back served both sexes in
this old mining town.*
Nick Cedar

93

KOOTENAI NATIONAL
FOREST, MONTANA

*In addition to the beautiful
mountains beyond, this privy
offers a view of Garver
Mountain fire tower. The
adjacent log cabin was built
in 1929; the tower went up
in 1963, replacing a prior one
built in 1932.* Jim Umhoefer

95

OUTHOUSE SONGS

They passed an ordinance
in the town
That said we'd have to tear it down—
That little brown shack out
back so dear to me
Though the health
department said
Its day was over and dead
It will stand forever
in my memory
Don't let 'em tear that
little brown building down
Don't let 'em tear that
little brown building down
Don't let 'em tear that
little brown building down
There's not another like it in
the country or the town.

— "Ode to the Little Brown Shack,"
by Billy Ed Wheeler,
from the singing of Ed Britt

GEM PEAK, MONTANA

The trip to the john is scenic for
visitors to this outhouse near
Gem Peak, Montana.
Jim Umhoefer

BEARTOOTH HIGHWAY,
MONTANA/WYOMING
*Motorists on the Beartooth
Highway don't get many
modern-day conveniences.
The tradeoff for this privy's
users, though, is the wonderful
panoramic view.*
Jim Umhoefer

*All changes, even the most longed for, have their melancholy;
for what we leave behind us is a part of ourselves;
we must die to one life before we can enter another.*

— Anatole France

97

NEW JERSEY

*This freshly painted outhouse
in the Pennsylvania woods
uses the crescent symbol,
but not in a typical moon
orientation. Placement
here serves as a window
for a privy visitor.*
William G. Simmonds

98

CHAPTER FOUR

Privy to a Phenom

As society on the whole, we're all probably pretty happy that most Americans don't have a functioning outhouse in their own backyards any more. But even though we cherish the best of modern conveniences, we never stray far from romanticizing the lives of those who first settled the American frontier.

Even if it's just to remember a piece of our own childhoods, our society has fallen in love with the old stinky shack out back. Many people relish their glimpses of yesteryear, so much so that they incorporate them into their modern living spaces and lives.

As a result, the outhouse has reached a new level in its popularity. Many of today's interior designs for the bathroom, in fact, focus on pastoral scenes surrounding privies of old. Whether it's wallpaper borders, textiles, hanging decor, or accessories, outhouse life is back, making a visit to those peaceful olden days a breeze. That is, for those who believe a breath of fresh air can come from the outhouse.

So how can we be so fascinated with such a distasteful, albeit necessary, part of our own subsistence? After all, most reminiscences of outhouse life by those who have really lived it are bittersweet at best.

Maybe it's because the truest form of the outhouse's existence is just that—a memory. And none of us want our memories to fade, especially the nostalgic ones.

THINKING OUTSIDE THE BOX

The Wachusett Area Rotary Club in Holden, Massachusetts, builds a new outhouse for its members and townspeople every year during the bitter-cold month of January.

Why? Because the darn things just keep sinking through the ice again. In fact, everyone's betting on it! For a $5 raffle, anyone can pick the day, month, and exact time (down to the second) that the annual outhouse will break through the ice and make someone a little richer. The 2005 winner nabbed $2,500 when the outhouse broke the ice on March 17 at 1:05:21 p.m., nearly two weeks later than the year before.

Interested parties can track the unfortunate loo's doomsday countdown on the Internet at the club's live web cam. The camera is set up to monitor the outhouse's every moment above ground and, most likely, to protect it from an untimely demise at the hands of local pranksters or greedy competitors.

The Rotary Club even offers the plans to the outhouse's construction, a materials lists, and the formula for weight-bearing capacity of ice on its website, to give contestants a fair shot. The town's "You Bet Your Ice" is a game of chance grounded in science. Contestants use the information provided to make an educated guess. You can, too. But with sold-out tickets promising so many eager participants to be a winner, don't bet the farm on it.

ONTARIO, WISCONSIN
Otherwise matching outhouses featuring moon and star windows join an old haywagon in the dairy-country sun.
Jim Umhoefer

PORCUPINE CREEK,
MONTANA

*Ranches can get quite large,
making a strategically
placed outhouse an
important property asset.*
Jim Umhoefer

*Restored and moved to a
park in a historic village,
this brick privy stands as a
symbol of a simpler time.*
William G. Simmonds

*It's never safe to be nostalgic about something until you're
absolutely certain there's no chance of it coming back.*

— Bill Vaughn

*Beautiful fall colors surround
this white privy on the grounds
of Trauger's Farm Market
in eastern Pennsylvania.
The stone building beyond is
typical of early Pennsylvania
farm structures.*
William G. Simmonds

FRANKENMUTH, MICHIGAN
*Outhouse kitsch encompasses
many products, including these
unique miniature outhouses
constructed and sold by
Redbeard's Antiques and
Collectibles. The license plates
above the doors give a good
sense of their scale.*
William G. Simmonds

UPSTATE NEW YORK

A wreath is a common adornment for an outhouse door. This privy has one, but the privy itself also serves as a decorative yard ornament.
William G. Simmonds

RANDSBURG,
CALIFORNIA

A coat of barn paint gives this tin outhouse a more welcoming appearance. The clear ground around it suggests it's in regular service. Nick Cedar

Ironically, rural America has become viewed by a growing number of Americans as having a higher quality of life not because of what it has, but rather because of what it does not have!

— Don A. Dillman

MESOPOTAMIA, OHIO

This two-seat outhouse was built in 1891. It is currently filled with garden supplies. Future plans call for a fresh coat of paint and a move to the garden, where it will become a decorative centerpiece.
William G. Simmonds

111

One Man's Trash

For nearly two decades, *Antique Bottle & Glass Collector* magazine out of East Greenville, Pennsylvania, has given glass and bottle hobbyists tips-of-the-trade on everything from how to find these buried treasures to bottle identification and information on nationwide showing circuits and glass auctions. One of the subjects that often comes up is how treasure hunters found loot that was buried deep in privy pits.

The seemingly rough-and-ready art of privy digging actually requires a heightened sense of awareness of some of the more well-respected cultural sciences of our times, such as history, geography, and geology, as well as social and political science.

For example, Civil War enthusiasts have always known the outhouse treasure trove exists, based solely on their knowledge of the civilian way of life around the 1860s.

During that time, many families passed down china, coins, gold, jewelry, porcelain, and other prized possessions through the generations. In fact, it was not that uncommon for even the poorest of families, especially rural farmers and westward-bound settler types, to own a small stash of valuables. These were treasures brought to America from faraway motherlands and were cherished as much for their priceless heirloom worth as their tremendous monetary merit.

These precious pieces of family history were rarely parted with by choice. But during the war, many families had to ditch their only riches to save them from being stolen by plundering troops from the North and South.

Preservation of family history was the idea behind hiding such bounty in the outhouse pit. It was a place that not even the most unscrupulous infantry man wanted to sully around in, looking for booty.

John O'Dell, a man of much privy-digging fame as a bottle book publisher and connoisseur of all types of antique bottles, notes the following on his website: "The pattern we privy diggers see mirrors . . . history. The archaeological evidence we've uncovered shows most nineteenth-century dwellings did not have indoor plumbing, although we occasionally find a property for which no outdoor privy can be located.

"Beginning around the mid-1850s, a few finer homes had built-in 'bathrooms.' Around the turn of the century we find 'flushers,' outdoor toilets with clay or iron-drainpipes leading into an underground vault, an underground brick structure plastered on the inside that had an exit drain tile near the top. Sometimes flushers were built right on top of older holes, the older hole serving as the septic tank.

"We often find clay tiles intruding into the earlier privy wall. These tiles, generally put in around the turn of the century, served as an overflow mechanism from the privy hole to the newly built sewers at the street. We regularly find privies, judging from the artifacts, that were still being used well into the twentieth century."

He also writes that many of the former outhouse holes contain screw-top bottles bearing the inscription "Federal law prohibits the reuse or resale of this bottle." These bottles, dating from well into the 1930s, are most often found in rural areas where waste disposal methods took longer to update.

While O'Dell often finds bottles worth good money in outhouses, he's digging for more than a cash bonus. So is Eddie Brater, who runs an easy-to-remember website out of New Haven, Ohio—www.privydigger.com. He describes his motto for wading through the muck as his way to dig up the past, one yard at a time. It's easier to understand the passion that Eddie and others like him often have for their chosen pursuit when you read Eddie's self-proclaimed purpose for being a privy-digger. It reads:

> I am dedicated to the ethical rescue and preservation of items thrown into the time capsules that were the outhouse pits of the nineteenth century. It seems that it was a very common practice to use the outhouse pit as one of the main garbage receptacles. I and my associates excavate these old outhouse pits to reclaim the glass bottles and other artifacts that were tossed in as garbage.
>
> Contrary to most first impressions, there is no bad smell, no germs, and no bacteria. Mother Nature has turned all the biological contents back into pure earth compost. We do not dig up the privy pits that still have the outhouse building on top of them. We use metal probes that we push into the ground to look for tell-tale signs like soft spots and the crunch of deep glass. Most homes built before 1880 have two to four already filled-in old outhouse pits.
>
> . . . Once we find a pit, we lay down a plastic tarp and carefully cut the sod into a 4 [foot] by 4 [foot] area. Then we cut that into 1 by 1 foot squares, and move them to the tarp where they are re-assembled. We then place another large plastic tarp on the ground at the edge of the hole to put the dirt on. As we dig, the dirt pile becomes larger. Pits run from 4 to 10 feet deep and take just one day to dig and refill. After we have reached the bottom and retrieved all the artifacts, we refill the pit, carefully packing it every two feet or so. We then replace the sod and water it in. You can hardly tell we were even there.

Eddie also has an ongoing online auction of his wares. The items for sale include a long list of some other man's trash, which include some of the following items:

Antique bottles
Trade, tavern, reed, or face pipes
Antique bisque doll heads
Antique marbles
Antique jars
Stoneware
Chamber pots

FRANKENMUTH,
MICHIGAN

*Surrounded by beautiful
flowers, this outhouse stands
tall at Grandpa Tiny's Farm
and Petting Zoo just outside
of Frankenmuth, Michigan.*
William G. Simmonds

*Nostalgia is the longing to go back to the good old
days when you were neither good nor old.*

*Dated 1820, this carved
gravestone must be among the
oldest in Michigan. Cemetery
visitors here have use
of a shaded privy.*
William G. Simmonds

MESOPOTAMIA, OHIO
A men's/ladies' outhouse behind a meeting hall in Trumbull County, Ohio. This community is largely Amish, many of whom still live without indoor plumbing.
William G. Simmonds

In back of the Rural Dale United Methodist Church is this great old two-seater. It serves nature in more than the usual way by sheltering a bird's nest under its eaves.
William G. Simmonds

CULTURAL ICON

Open since mid-2002, The Rossignol Cultural Centre houses on the only North American history museum of its kind—the Museum of the Outhouse.

Located in Liverpool, Nova Scotia, Canada, the Rossignol is a 24,000-square-foot renovated school house that now houses the lifelong personal and solicited collections of Canadian Sherman Hines, a longtime professional photographer and author of more than 10 highly visual outhouse books.

Purportedly, Hines started visually documenting outhouses after a conversation he had with an elderly lady, who lived in the oldest remaining house in Mill Village, Nova Scotia. While the two had tea, the woman apparently told Hines she believed he should document all the outhouses left in the area before they were gone. So he started by photographing hers.

Then, over the next handful of years, as a friendly joke, he sent her a card every Christmas with a photo of another outhouse.

Soon the thought of some day creating an entire photo book moved him to photograph every outhouse he could find during 1977 and 1978, which resulted in *Outhouses of the East*. Two more books eventually followed.

His photographs, along with more than 3,000 artifacts and collectibles, fill The Museum of the Outhouse portion of the cultural center (which also houses a folk art museum; an apothecary [old-time drug store] museum; a hunting, fishing and guide-sporting museum; and a wildlife museum).

As a finishing touch, the Rossignol also has a gift shop where visitors can buy a bit of anything outhouse, including gifts, books, postcards, and other mementos of this vanishing folk icon.

Visitors also can create their own place in outhouse history. For $25 a brick, anyone can add their name to the museum's "Wall of Fame"—part of the brick outhouses there.

With all of its oddities, it's no wonder that the Museum of the Outhouse has become one of the top 10 tourist destinations on the Northeast's famed Lighthouse Route.

*In time, the outhouse tucked
among the other farm buildings
will be just a memory—not
because it served a need that
no longer exists, but because
better, cleaner, more convenient
means have been developed
to answer nature's call.*
William G. Simmonds

This homeowner has a real fascination with collecting outhouses, and not the cutesy indoor decorative kind. No, Mary Lou collects real outhouses. She currently has seven lining her backyard. She also has a very understanding husband, Paul.

William G. Simmonds

NORTH BLOOMFIELD,
CALIFORNIA

*Though primitive inside,
this outhouse's exterior is
in clean, solid shape.*
Nick Cedar

Half the pleasure of recalling the past lies in the editing.

*Pans, a lantern, a cheese grater,
and a doorknob are among
the knick-knacks accumulating
by the loo. Are they just
decorations or perhaps
reminders of chores that
need to be done?* Nick Cedar

LIZ BUTTE, IDAHO

*A worn path lets hikers and
bicyclists in the Liz Butte
area know that this privy
is open for business.*
Jim Umhoefer

INDEX